# WOMEN IN SCIENCE & TECHNOLOGY

# Grace HOPPER

BY JAN FIELDS
ILLUSTRATED BY ELENA BIA

Rourke
Educational Media
rourkeeducationalmedia.com

A Division of
Carson
Dellosa
Education

# ROURKE'S
# SCHOOL to HOME
### CONNECTIONS
# BEFORE AND DURING READING ACTIVITIES

## Before Reading: *Building Background Knowledge and Vocabulary*

Building background knowledge can help children process new information and build upon what they already know. Before reading a book, it is important to tap into what children already know about the topic. This will help them develop their vocabulary and increase their reading comprehension.

### Questions and Activities to Build Background Knowledge:

1. Look at the front cover of the book and read the title. What do you think this book will be about?
2. What do you already know about this topic?
3. Take a book walk and skim the pages. Look at the table of contents, photographs, captions, and bold words. Did these text features give you any information or predictions about what you will read in this book?

## Vocabulary: *Vocabulary Is Key to Reading Comprehension*

Use the following directions to prompt a conversation about each word.

- Read the vocabulary words.
- What comes to mind when you see each word?
- What do you think each word means?

### Vocabulary Words:
- code
- determination
- digital
- languages
- non-combat
- physics
- programmers
- wealthy

## During Reading: *Reading for Meaning and Understanding*

To achieve deep comprehension of a book, children are encouraged to use close reading strategies. During reading, it is important to have children stop and make connections. These connections result in deeper analysis and understanding of a book.

 Close Reading a Text

During reading, have children stop and talk about the following:

- Any confusing parts
- Any unknown words
- Text to text, text to self, text to world connections
- The main idea in each chapter or heading

Encourage children to use context clues to determine the meaning of any unknown words. These strategies will help children learn to analyze the text more thoroughly as they read.

When you are finished reading this book, turn to the next-to-last page for **Text-Dependent Questions** and an **Extension Activity**.

# TABLE OF CONTENTS

# CURIOUS GRACE

Grace Hopper was born on December 9, 1906. Her parents encouraged her to read, to discover, and to face problems without quitting. Grace was good at all of those things. She especially loved reading. Her family often found her on the steps of their New York City home with her nose in a book.

When Grace was seven she became curious about clocks. She took the family clocks apart to learn how they worked. Grace wasn't punished for her clock destruction. Her mother admired her **determination** and curiosity.

When Grace was ready for college, she had a problem. Her math scores were high, but her Latin scores were too low. Grace did not give up. She studied and tried again. She made it into Vassar College.

Grace graduated from Vassar with top honors in math and **physics**. Grace wanted to learn more. She went to study math at Yale University.

In the 1930s, **wealthy** young women often went to college. But women were not really welcome at Yale. From 1934 to 1937, only one woman earned a doctorate in math at Yale. It was Grace.

After graduating, Grace became a college professor. She taught her students to see how math is part of everything.

Grace enjoyed teaching, but her focus changed when the United States went to war. During World War II, women could volunteer to serve in **non-combat** roles. Grace wanted to serve her country, but she was too old and did not weigh enough to join the Navy. Grace did not give up. She received special permission. She joined the U.S. Naval Reserve and became an officer.

**Wartime WAVES**

Grace joined the Navy's volunteer branch called the WAVES (Women Accepted for Volunteer Emergency Service). More than 83,000 women served in the WAVES during the war.

You'll be happy too, and feel so proud serving as a **WAVE** in the Navy.

# GRACE MEETS THE COMPUTER

The Navy needed Grace's math skills. Harvard University had a new computer that could solve problems for the Navy. But they needed computer programmers who could think in new ways.

The Mark I was the first **digital** computer. It was huge! It didn't have a mouse or a keyboard. The computer read its instructions from a long piece of paper with holes punched in it. Once it worked out a problem, the Mark I typed the answer on an automatic typewriter. It worked slowly, running day and night making calculations.

The Navy **programmers** had to help teach the Mark I to solve problems. They broke down the steps and wrote the directions in notebooks. Grace noticed that the same steps were part of many tasks. She saved those steps in a notebook to make finding and using them easier and faster.

Over time, new computers were imagined and built. Grace worked on the Mark II and the Mark III. Then she left active duty in the Navy. She worked at Harvard University on faster, smaller computers.

**A Computer Bug**
Once when the Mark II stopped working, Grace found a moth caught inside the computer. She thought it was funny to find a real "computer bug." She taped the moth in her log book.

# ALWAYS A TEACHER

The earliest computers only understood numbers. They followed commands given in number form. It was hard for people to learn to think like a computer. Grace thought computers needed to learn human **languages**. She taught the computer to recognize some words as commands to run common bits of **code**. This made programming easier and faster. Grace wanted computers to learn more. She and her team invented FLOW-MATIC, a computer language that used many normal words.

UNIVAC FLOW-MATIC

*by Remington Rand Univac*

Programmers invented more languages. Grace thought a single language needed to work for most computers. The language that worked best was called COBOL. Grace didn't invent COBOL, but she helped convince people to use it.

Because of this work, the Navy called on Grace again. She taught people in the Navy how to use COBOL. Grace served in the Navy as a teacher and computer expert for 19 more years. She finally retired at age 79 as a rear admiral. She was the oldest serving officer in the military.

Grace appeared on television and in magazines. She won awards. But Grace said her greatest work was teaching young people to look for new ways to do things.

"Humans are allergic to change. They love to say, 'We've always done it this way.' I try to fight that," Grace once said.

# TIME LINE

**1906:** Grace Brewster Murray is born on December 9 in New York City.

**1924:** Grace is accepted into Vassar College.

**1928:** Grace earns a degree in mathematics and physics from Vassar.

**1928:** Grace enters graduate school at Yale University.

**1930:** Grace marries Vincent Foster Hopper.

**1934:** Grace receives a PhD in mathematics from Yale University.

**1943:** Grace joins the U.S. Naval Reserve.

**1944:** Grace is promoted to lieutenant junior grade.

**1946:** Grace is released from active duty because of her age.

**1952**: Grace develops the first computer compiler, the A-O System.

**1963:** Grace is awarded the Legion of Merit by Congress for her outstanding service to the military.

**1966:** Grace is forced to retire again.

**1967:** The U.S. Navy needs Grace's help again.

**1969:** Grace is the first person named "Computer Science Man of the Year" by the Data Processing Management Association.

**1973:** Grace is promoted to the rank of captain.

**1985:** Grace is promoted to rear admiral.

**1986:** Grace retires from the U.S. Navy again at the age of 79.

**1991:** Grace receives the National Medal of Technology—the first individual woman to receive this highest honor in engineering and technology in the United States.

**1992:** Grace dies in her sleep at 85 years old.

**1995:** A U.S. Navy warship is named after Grace, the USS *Hopper.*

**1998:** U.S. Navy awards Grace the Acquisition Pioneer Award for visionary and innovative leadership.

**2004:** To honor Grace, the University of Missouri creates a computer museum, dubbed "Grace's Place."

**2016:** President Barack Obama awards Grace the Presidential Medal of Freedom.

# GLOSSARY

**code** (kode): instructions for making a computer work that are written in a computer language

**determination** (di-tur-muh-NAY-shuhn): a strong drive to accomplish something

**digital** (DIJ-i-tuhl): based on information stored and understood in a form using only the numbers 0 and 1

**languages** (LANG-gwij-iz): systems of words, signs, or symbols used to express ideas

**non-combat** (non-KAHM-bat): related to military service that does not involve fighting

**physics** (FIZ-iks): the science of matter and energy and how they interact to make heat, light, electricity, and sound

**programmers** (PROH-gram-urz): people whose job is to write instructions for computers to follow

**wealthy** (WEL-thee): having far above the average amount of money

# INDEX

# TEXT-DEPENDENT QUESTIONS

1. How did Grace's life show that she didn't give up easily?

2. Why did Grace begin working with computers?

3. Which branch of the U.S. Navy did Grace volunteer to serve?

4. How was the Mark I different from modern computers?

5. Why did Grace want to change how computers understood commands?

# EXTENSION ACTIVITY

Computer programs are made up of lists of small tasks that lead to the final result. Imagine you receive a robot that can help you with any chore, but you must create a computer program telling the robot how to do it. The robot understands words but doesn't know how to do anything. How would you break down your task into many clear steps? Write a program to get your new robot to do the chore.

## ABOUT THE AUTHOR

Jan Fields has written dozens of fiction and nonfiction books for young readers. She's tracked down interesting information on subjects ranging from movie making to legendary monsters. She lives with her husband in New England, surrounded by history.

## ABOUT THE ILLUSTRATOR

Elena Bia was born in a little town in northern Italy, near the Alps. In her free time, she puts her heart into personal comics. She also loves walking on the beach and walking through the woods. For her, flowers are the most beautiful form of life.

© 2020 Rourke Educational Media

www.rourkeeducationalmedia.com

Quote sources: Gist, Shelley. 2019. "WHM: Grace Hopper - Carolina Women's Center". Carolina Women's Center. https://womenscenter.unc.edu/2017/03/whm-grace-hopper/

Edited by: Kim Thompson
Cover and interior design by: Rhea Magaro-Wallace

**Library of Congress PCN Data**

Grace Hopper / Jan Fields
 (Women in Science and Technology)
  ISBN 978-1-73161-430-8 (hard cover)
  ISBN 978-1-73161-225-0 (soft cover)
  ISBN 978-1-73161-535-0 (e-Book)
  ISBN 978-1-73161-640-1 (ePub)
Library of Congress Control Number: 2019932136

Rourke Educational Media
Printed in the United States of America,
North Mankato, Minnesota